What is a Welshman?

What is a Welshman?
R S Thomas

Christopher Davies

Contents

He lives here

and he showed it to me
 and I recognised it
 by its smell the smell of chapels
   gone sour
 and I said God deliver me
   from the womb that is stubborn
to bear
 and I lay on the bleak hills
 black with the dust of coal
 not yet mined and they stood round
   with white faces
and the old familiar slang
of the valleys was on the lips
   of the wind
 welcome boi bach
fallen among the slag and clinkers
of time with a language
   filched from the dictionary
   of the tribes we await
your sermon
 and a pulpit grew up under my feet
 and I climbed into it and
it was the cage
of the mine-shaft down down down
   to preach to the lost souls
   of the coal-face reminding
how green is the childhood
   of a glib people taunting
 them with the abandonment
 of the national for the class struggle

If you can call it living

In Wales there are
no crocodiles, but the tears
continue to flow from
their slimed sources. Women
with white hair and strawberry
faces peer at you from behind
curtains; wobbling sopranos
split the chapels; the clerks undress
the secretaries with
their lean eyes.
                    Who will employ
the loafers at the street
corners, choking over
the joke's phlegm?
                    Anything to
sell? cries the tourist
to the native rummaging among
the remnants of his self-respect.

Somewhere to go for a laugh

I am not from these parts.
My auntie's is the next house
but one in the next village
but one in the next
county. If you hear me use
English, it is not for you to judge
the accent. I have ways, too,
of getting about; my nose tells
the seasons, as your calendars do.
I am more equal; in twelve towns
under the grinding of the shillings
I have heard the muse purr. My father
was after all one of those born
to preferment—Rural Dean
of the Bottom Hundred I have known him called.

He has the vote

and a stupendous future
awaits this little—

    VOTE TORY—this little
nation of . . . . What does crachach
mean?
    (Every drop
        of water is worth its weight
        in tears, but they are running
        out now like the variations on
        the cynghanedd.)
                VOTE
LABOUR and protect
your class. There is an aristocracy
of the pit, too.
        VOTE LIBERAL
and allow England to enjoy
your prospects.
        VOTE PLAID, mun
and be dammed for your own sake.

To pay for his keep

So this was on the way
to a throne! He looked round
at the perspiring ranks
of ageing respectables:
police, tradesmen, councillors,
rigid with imagined
loyalty; and beyond them at
the town with its mean streets and
pavements filthy with
dog shit.
        The castle was
huge. All that dead weight
of the past, that overloading
of the law's mounting
equipment! A few medals
would do now. He permitted
himself a small smile,
sipping at it in the mind's
coolness.
        And never noticed,
because of the dust raised
by the prayers of the fagged
clergy, that far hill
in the sun with the long line
of its trees climbing
it like a procession
of young people, young as himself.

He lies down to be counted

And in Tregaron Henry Richard
still freezes, cast in shame to preside
over the pacifism of a servile people.

Thomas Charles, too, has seen the Bible
petrified. Nothing can stir the pages
of the book he holds; not even the draught from Tryweryn.

In our country you make your way
from monument to monument. Besides
the villages' and the towns'

statues, there are the memories of those others
who gave their lives for the freedom
to make money, the innumerable Joneses

and Owens, who might have brought our blood
to the boil; who are clothed now
in the indiscriminate mufti of the soil.

On a diet of warmed-up music

His favourite instrument
the harmonium—such breathless
music! When asthma
afflicts the arts, what

hope for the prosaic
millions, whose search is
for strings to pull? He once
had the harp, the goddess

with gold ribs; but long
ago now her feathers
were plucked. By an old hearth's
ashes she sits and shivers.

He is sometimes contrary

No poem to be dialled?

No, I wouldn't help.
I was not available
to you for two new pence . . . .

If I told you that Catraeth
has always to be re-fought;
that the birds of Rhiannon
will never be heard in your
suburban garden; that office hours
are the best time to pluck trout
from the silver branches of the streams
of Mawddwy. If I brought thirst
upon you that the dusty beer
of your addiction could not
allay . . .
How would that have comforted you?

His condescensions are short-lived

I don't know, he said. I feel sorry
for the English—a fine people
in some ways, but victims
of their traditions. All those tanks
and guns; the processions
that go nowhere; the medals
and gold braid; the government's
yearly awards; the replenishment
of the clapped ranks of
the peerage. Democracy is the tip
the rich and the well-born give
for your homage.
        I admired him
there, as he sat nonchalantly
in his chair, flicking the ash from
his cigarette—supplied, by the way,
as most things in Wales are
supplied, by English wholesalers.

The earth does its best for him

The paintings are under glass,
or in dry rooms it is difficult
to breathe in; they are tired
of returning the hard stare
of eyes. The sculptures are smooth
from familiarity. There is a smell
of dust, the precipitation
of culture from dead skies.

I return to Lleyn,
repository of the condescension
of time. Through the car's
open windows the scent of hay
comes. It is incense, the seasonally
renewed offering of the live earth.

He agrees with Henry Ford

Llywelyn? Old hat.
Glyndwr? A con man,
Iolo licking his arse
for a doublet, for his next
meal.
      Rusty their armour,
yellow their bones, let them
brag in the safety of the dry
libraries. Honours forbid
that they should start their nonsense.

Rising sixty, my post-war
credits are due, my feet
are towards the electric
fire; my favourite programme
begins. I have drawn the curtains
on the raw sky where our history
bleeds, where Cilgwri's ousel
on my ramshackle aerial
keeps the past's goal
against the balls of to-morrow.

It hurts him to think

The decree went forth
     to destroy the language—'not cariad'
they said, 'love'. The nursing future
     saw the tightening lips
of the English drawn on the hard sky
     to the east. 'You can have the job,
if you ask for it in the right
     words'. 'Come buy, come buy',
tolled the bells of the churches
     in the new towns. The Welsh
put on their best clothes
     and took their produce
to market, and brought it back
     with them, unsold. 'We want
nothing from you but your
     land'. The heiresses fell
for the velvet businessmen
     of the shires. The peasantry
saw their pastures fenced in
     with the bones of heroes. The
industrialists came, burrowing
     in the corpse of a nation
for its congealed blood. I was
     born into the squalor of
their feeding and sucked their speech
     in with my mother's
infected milk, so that whatever
     I throw up now is still theirs.

FIRST IMPRESSION 1974
SECOND IMPRESSION 1978
THIRD IMPRESSION 1986

Published by
Christopher Davies (Publishers) Ltd.,
P.O. Box 403, Sketty,
Swansea, SA2 9BE.

ISBN 0 7154 0067 3

*Printed in Wales by
Dynevor Printing Company,
Rawlings Road,
Llandybïe, Dyfed.*